Table Of Contents

01

Chapter 1: Introduction to Artificial Intelligence

What is Artificial Intelligence?

In this subchapter, we will delve into the fascinating realm of Artificial Intelligence (AI) and explore its various facets. As technology continues to advance at an unprecedented pace, AI has emerged as one of the most transformative fields, captivating the attention of people from all walks of life. Whether you are a seasoned professional or simply a curious mind over 30, this section of the book, "AI Mastery: A Guide for the Curious 30+ Mind," will provide you with a comprehensive understanding of AI and its applications.

Artificial Intelligence refers to the development of computer systems that possess the ability to perform tasks that typically require human intelligence. These tasks include understanding natural language, recognizing images, making decisions, and even learning from experience. AI encompasses a broad spectrum of technologies, including machine learning algorithms, neural networks, intelligent virtual assistants, and deep learning.

Machine learning algorithms are at the heart of AI. They enable computers to learn from data without being explicitly programmed. By identifying patterns and making predictions or decisions based on those patterns, these algorithms can perform complex tasks with remarkable accuracy. From recommending movies on streaming platforms to detecting fraudulent transactions, machine learning algorithms have become an integral part of our daily lives.

Neural networks, inspired by the human brain, play a pivotal role in AI. These networks consist of interconnected nodes, or artificial neurons, that process and transmit information. By simulating the neural connections in our brains, neural networks excel at tasks such as image and speech recognition, natural language processing, and even autonomous driving.

Intelligent virtual assistants, like Siri and Alexa, have become household names, exemplifying the practical applications of AI. These assistants utilize AI technologies to understand voice commands, answer questions, and perform various tasks, making our lives more convenient and efficient.

Deep learning, a subset of machine learning, has gained significant traction in recent years. It involves training neural networks on vast amounts of data to recognize intricate patterns and make predictions. Deep learning has revolutionized fields like computer vision, natural language processing, and robotics, propelling AI to new heights.

As we navigate the ever-evolving landscape of AI, it is crucial to understand its immense potential and the ethical considerations it raises. This subchapter aims to equip you with the foundational knowledge needed to grasp the intricacies of AI and appreciate its transformative impact on society.

Brief History of Artificial Intelligence

During the 1960s and 1970s, AI researchers focused on developing expert systems that could solve complex problems by reasoning and applying logical rules. This era witnessed the birth of intelligent virtual assistants that could understand natural language and provide answers to user queries.

The 1980s and 1990s saw a shift towards more practical applications of AI, such as voice recognition, image processing, and robotics. Neural networks gained attention again with the development of deep learning algorithms, which enabled machines to learn from large datasets and make predictions with incredible accuracy.

The early 2000s marked the rise of intelligent virtual assistants like Siri and Alexa, which utilized AI technologies to understand and respond to user commands. This breakthrough brought AI into the mainstream, making it accessible to a broader audience.

In recent years, AI has witnessed exponential growth due to advancements in computing power and the availability of vast amounts of data. Deep learning, in particular, has revolutionized fields like computer vision, natural language processing, and autonomous vehicles.

Today, AI is permeating almost every aspect of our lives, from personalized recommendations on online platforms to self-driving cars. The potential of AI is vast, with ongoing research and development in areas such as reinforcement learning, generative adversarial networks, and explainable AI.

Importance of Artificial Intelligence in Today's World

In today's rapidly evolving world, the importance of Artificial Intelligence (AI) cannot be overstated. AI has emerged as a transformative technology that is revolutionizing various industries and enhancing our daily lives. This subchapter explores the significance of AI in today's world, focusing on the niches of Artificial Intelligence, Machine learning algorithms, Neural networks, Intelligent virtual assistants, and Deep learning.

Artificial Intelligence, at its core, refers to the simulation of human intelligence in machines that can perform tasks that typically require human intelligence. It encompasses a wide range of technologies and applications, including machine learning algorithms, neural networks, intelligent virtual assistants, and deep learning.

One of the primary reasons why AI is essential in today's world is its ability to process vast amounts of data at an unprecedented speed. Machine learning algorithms enable computers to learn from data, identify patterns, and make predictions or decisions based on the analyzed information. This has tremendous implications across various industries such as healthcare, finance, and transportation, where data-driven decision-making is crucial for success.

Neural networks, a subset of AI, are modeled after the human brain and are capable of recognizing complex patterns and correlations. Their ability to process unstructured data, such as images or natural language, has revolutionized fields like computer vision and natural language processing. Neural networks have enabled breakthroughs in facial recognition, speech recognition, and even autonomous vehicles.

Intelligent virtual assistants, powered by AI, have become ubiquitous in our lives. These assistants, such as Siri, Alexa, or Google Assistant, can understand and respond to voice commands, perform tasks, and provide valuable information. They have transformed the way we interact with technology, making our lives more convenient and efficient.

Deep learning, another subset of AI, has emerged as a powerful tool for solving complex problems. By utilizing neural networks with multiple layers, deep learning algorithms can automatically learn hierarchical representations of data. This has led to advancements in areas like image and speech recognition, natural language processing, and even drug discovery.

In conclusion, the importance of Artificial Intelligence in today's world cannot be understated. From machine learning algorithms and neural networks to intelligent virtual assistants and deep learning, AI is transforming industries and enhancing our lives in countless ways. As individuals over 30, it is crucial to understand and embrace AI to navigate the ever-evolving technological landscape effectively. Whether it's benefiting from data-driven decisions or leveraging intelligent virtual assistants, AI has the potential to unlock new opportunities and improve the quality of our lives.

02

Chapter 2: Understanding Machine Learning Algorithms

Introduction to Machine Learning

Machine learning is a fascinating field within the realm of artificial intelligence that has revolutionized the way we solve complex problems and make decisions. In this subchapter, we will delve into the fundamentals of machine learning, providing an accessible introduction to this exciting discipline. Whether you are a tech-savvy individual over 30 or a curious mind keen to explore the world of artificial intelligence, this subchapter will serve as a comprehensive guide.

Machine learning algorithms lie at the heart of this field, enabling computers to learn from data and make accurate predictions or decisions without being explicitly programmed. By leveraging the power of data, these algorithms can uncover patterns, relationships, and insights that may not be apparent to humans. As an over 30's audience interested in artificial intelligence, understanding machine learning algorithms is crucial to comprehending the potential and limitations of AI systems.

Neural networks, a subset of machine learning algorithms, have gained significant attention in recent years due to their ability to mimic the human brain's structure and functioning. These networks consist of interconnected nodes, or artificial neurons, that process and transmit information. Neural networks have enabled breakthroughs in various domains, such as image and speech recognition, natural language processing, and intelligent virtual assistants like Siri and Alexa.

Deep learning is a powerful technique within machine learning that utilizes neural networks with multiple layers, enabling computers to extract higher-level representations from raw data. This advancement has led to significant improvements in computer vision, autonomous vehicles, and even medical diagnosis. As an over 30's audience interested in artificial intelligence, understanding deep learning will allow you to appreciate the immense potential it holds for transforming various industries.

In this subchapter, we will explore the practical applications of machine learning, including its use in healthcare, finance, marketing, and more. We will discuss the ethical considerations associated with machine learning, such as bias and privacy concerns, emphasizing the importance of responsible AI development.

By the end of this subchapter, you will have a solid understanding of the foundations of machine learning, its algorithms, neural networks, deep learning, and their practical applications. Armed with this knowledge, you will be better equipped to navigate the rapidly evolving world of artificial intelligence and make informed decisions about its implementation in your personal and professional life.

Whether you are a seasoned professional or a curious individual, this subchapter is designed to satisfy your hunger for knowledge in the field of artificial intelligence and machine learning. So, let's embark on this exciting journey together and unlock the mysteries of intelligent machines.

Supervised Learning

In the vast world of Artificial Intelligence (AI), one of the most powerful and widely-used techniques is known as supervised learning. This subchapter will delve into the intricacies of supervised learning and provide a comprehensive understanding of its applications in various fields.

Supervised learning is a type of machine learning algorithm that involves training an AI model using labeled data. The concept is simple yet effective – the model learns from previous examples to make accurate predictions or decisions when presented with new, unseen data.

The beauty of supervised learning lies in its versatility. It can be applied to numerous domains, from finance and healthcare to marketing and self-driving cars. By continually feeding the model with labeled data, it becomes increasingly proficient at recognizing patterns and making informed decisions.

Machine learning algorithms are at the core of supervised learning. These algorithms utilize mathematical and statistical techniques to analyze data, identify patterns, and make predictions. They can be classified into various types, such as regression, classification, and decision trees, each tailored to specific tasks.

One of the most significant breakthroughs in supervised learning is the development of neural networks. Inspired by the human brain, neural networks consist of interconnected nodes, or artificial neurons, that process information. They excel at tasks like image and speech recognition, natural language processing, and sentiment analysis.

Intelligent virtual assistants, like Siri and Alexa, are prime examples of how supervised learning has revolutionized our daily lives. These virtual assistants use machine learning algorithms to understand and respond to voice commands, providing us with personalized recommendations, weather updates, and much more.

Deep learning, a subset of machine learning, has also gained immense popularity due to its exceptional performance in various domains. It leverages neural networks with multiple layers, enabling the model to learn hierarchical representations of data. Deep learning has made significant strides in computer vision, autonomous driving, and even medical diagnosis.

As the field of supervised learning continues to evolve, it presents tremendous opportunities for innovation and growth. Whether you're an aspiring data scientist or a curious mind over 30, understanding supervised learning and its applications in AI is essential. This subchapter will equip you with the necessary knowledge to explore and leverage the power of supervised learning, unlocking new possibilities in the world of artificial intelligence.

Unsupervised Learning

In the vast landscape of artificial intelligence (AI) and machine learning algorithms, unsupervised learning stands out as a powerful technique that holds immense potential for revolutionizing various fields. In this subchapter, we will delve into the world of unsupervised learning and explore its applications in neural networks, deep learning, and intelligent virtual assistants.

Unsupervised learning is a branch of machine learning where the algorithms learn patterns and structure from unlabeled data. Unlike supervised learning, which relies on labeled data, unsupervised learning algorithms work without any prior knowledge or guidance. This makes it particularly useful in situations where obtaining labeled data is challenging or expensive.

One of the key applications of unsupervised learning is in neural networks. Neural networks mimic the human brain's structure, consisting of interconnected nodes known as neurons. Unsupervised learning algorithms can be used to train neural networks to recognize patterns, classify data, or generate new content. Through unsupervised learning, neural networks can uncover hidden structures and relationships within large datasets, enabling them to make more accurate predictions and decisions.

Deep learning, a subset of machine learning, heavily relies on unsupervised learning techniques. With deep learning, multiple layers of neural networks are stacked together, allowing the system to learn complex representations of the data. Unsupervised learning plays a crucial role in pre-training these deep neural networks, enabling them to automatically extract features from the data and perform tasks such as image recognition, speech recognition, and natural language processing.

Intelligent virtual assistants, such as Siri, Alexa, and Google Assistant, have become an integral part of our daily lives. These assistants use unsupervised learning algorithms to understand and respond to natural language queries. By analyzing vast amounts of text data, unsupervised learning algorithms can identify patterns, extract meaning, and generate appropriate responses, making these virtual assistants more intelligent and conversational.

As unsupervised learning continues to advance, it holds immense potential for various industries and niches. From healthcare and finance to transportation and entertainment, the applications of unsupervised learning are limitless. By uncovering hidden patterns and relationships within data, unsupervised learning algorithms can help businesses make better decisions, identify anomalies, and improve efficiency.

In conclusion, unsupervised learning plays a pivotal role in the field of artificial intelligence and machine learning algorithms. Its ability to learn from unlabeled data and uncover hidden patterns makes it a powerful tool for neural networks, deep learning, and intelligent virtual assistants. As the technology continues to evolve, the impact of unsupervised learning will become increasingly significant, transforming the way we interact with AI systems and unlocking new possibilities for innovation.

Reinforcement Learning

In the vast realm of Artificial Intelligence (AI), one particular technique has emerged as a game-changer: reinforcement learning. This powerful approach enables machines to learn and make decisions by interacting with their environment. In this subchapter, we will delve into the fascinating world of reinforcement learning, exploring its key concepts, applications, and implications.

Reinforcement learning is a branch of machine learning that focuses on training intelligent agents to maximize their performance in a given environment. It draws inspiration from how humans and animals learn through trial and error, by receiving feedback in the form of rewards or punishments. By using this feedback, an agent can iteratively improve its decision-making abilities.

At its core, reinforcement learning involves three major components: the agent, the environment, and the rewards. The agent is the learner or decision-maker, while the environment represents the external context with which the agent interacts. Rewards serve as the feedback mechanism, guiding the agent towards desirable outcomes. Through a process of exploration and exploitation, the agent learns the optimal actions to take in various situations to maximize its reward.

The applications of reinforcement learning are vast and ever-expanding. From autonomous vehicles navigating complex road networks to intelligent virtual assistants providing personalized recommendations, this technique has revolutionized various industries. It has been used to optimize energy management systems, enhance stock trading algorithms, and even develop strategies for playing games like chess and Go at superhuman levels.

Reinforcement learning techniques, such as deep Q-networks (DQNs) and policy gradients, have also paved the way for advancements in deep learning and neural networks. These algorithms have pushed the boundaries of AI, enabling machines to learn from raw sensory input and achieve state-of-the-art results in image recognition, natural language processing, and more.

As a curious mind over 30, understanding reinforcement learning opens up a plethora of opportunities. Whether you are an AI enthusiast, a business professional seeking to leverage AI technologies, or simply intrigued by the potential of intelligent systems, this knowledge will empower you to navigate the rapidly evolving landscape of AI.

In the following chapters, we will delve deeper into the algorithms, techniques, and practical applications of reinforcement learning. We will explore how to design reward structures, train agents using different approaches, and address the ethical considerations surrounding AI. By the end of this book, you will have gained a comprehensive understanding of reinforcement learning and its implications, equipping you to embrace the possibilities and challenges of this transformative technology.

Comparison of Different Machine Learning Algorithms

In the vast and ever-evolving field of artificial intelligence, machine learning algorithms play a crucial role in enabling intelligent systems to learn and adapt from data. These algorithms form the foundation of various applications, including neural networks, intelligent virtual assistants, and deep learning. As curious individuals over the age of 30, it is essential to understand the different machine learning algorithms to fully grasp the potential and impact of artificial intelligence.

1. Supervised Learning Algorithms: This category of algorithms learns from labeled data, where each example is associated with a known output. It includes decision trees, support vector machines, and random forests. Supervised learning is commonly used for tasks such as classification and regression, making it suitable for applications like image recognition and fraud detection.

2. Unsupervised Learning Algorithms: Unlike supervised learning, unsupervised learning algorithms learn from unlabeled data. They aim to identify patterns, relationships, and hidden structures within the data. Clustering algorithms, such as K-means and hierarchical clustering, fall under this category. Unsupervised learning is beneficial for tasks like customer segmentation and anomaly detection.

3. Reinforcement Learning Algorithms: Reinforcement learning algorithms learn through interaction with an environment, where they receive feedback in the form of rewards or penalties. They optimize their actions to maximize cumulative rewards. This type of learning is employed in autonomous vehicles, game playing, and robotics, where the algorithm learns from trial and error.

4. Neural Networks: Neural networks are a set of algorithms inspired by the human brain's structure and functioning. They consist of interconnected layers of artificial neurons, where each neuron processes information and passes it to the next layer. Neural networks excel in tasks such as image and speech recognition, natural language processing, and recommendation systems.

5. Deep Learning Algorithms: Deep learning is a subset of neural networks that involve multiple layers of artificial neurons, enabling them to learn complex patterns and hierarchies. Convolutional neural networks (CNNs) are widely used for image and video analysis, while recurrent neural networks (RNNs) are effective in sequential data analysis, such as language translation and sentiment analysis.

Understanding the strengths and weaknesses of different machine learning algorithms is crucial for selecting the appropriate approach for a given problem. While supervised learning offers precise predictions, unsupervised learning provides insights into data structures. Reinforcement learning enables autonomous decision-making, while neural networks and deep learning excel in complex pattern recognition tasks.

By delving into the comparison of these machine learning algorithms, we can unlock the potential of artificial intelligence in various domains. Whether it's developing intelligent virtual assistants, analyzing big data, or creating innovative solutions, a solid understanding of these algorithms will empower curious minds over the age of 30 to navigate the rapidly advancing world of AI with confidence and curiosity.

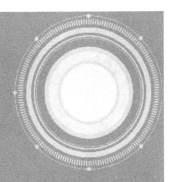

03

Chapter 3: Basics of Neural Networks

Introduction to Neural Networks

In this subchapter, we will delve into the fascinating world of neural networks, a fundamental aspect of artificial intelligence and machine learning algorithms. As we explore the concepts behind this powerful technology, we aim to provide a comprehensive understanding of neural networks and their applications, particularly in the realms of intelligent virtual assistants and deep learning.

Neural networks are computational models inspired by the structure and functionality of the human brain. Just as our brain consists of interconnected neurons, neural networks are composed of artificial neurons, also known as nodes or units. These nodes work collectively to process and analyze complex data, enabling the network to learn from patterns, make predictions, and perform intelligent tasks.

The significance of neural networks lies in their ability to recognize patterns and learn from vast amounts of data. This capability opens up a multitude of possibilities in various fields, including image and speech recognition, natural language processing, and recommendation systems. By employing neural networks, intelligent virtual assistants such as Siri, Alexa, and Google Assistant can understand and respond to our commands, making our lives more convenient and efficient.

Deep learning is a subset of neural networks that has gained immense popularity in recent years. It involves training neural networks with multiple hidden layers to process increasingly complex data. This methodology has revolutionized fields like computer vision, allowing us to develop accurate image recognition systems and self-driving cars.

Throughout this subchapter, we will explore the fundamental components of neural networks, including input and output layers, hidden layers, activation functions, and weight adjustments. We will discuss popular network architectures, such as feedforward neural networks, convolutional neural networks, and recurrent neural networks, highlighting their unique characteristics and applications.

Perceptron Model

Additionally, we will address the challenges and limitations of neural networks, such as overfitting, vanishing gradients, and the need for large datasets. Understanding these limitations is crucial for developing effective machine learning algorithms and optimizing neural network architectures.

By the end of this subchapter, you will have a solid foundation in neural networks, allowing you to appreciate their role in artificial intelligence and machine learning. Whether you are a curious individual exploring the world of AI or a professional seeking to enhance your knowledge in this field, this subchapter will equip you with the necessary insights to understand, utilize, and appreciate the power of neural networks.

The Perceptron Model is an essential concept in the field of Artificial Intelligence (AI), specifically within the domain of Machine Learning Algorithms. In this subchapter, we will delve into the intricacies of the Perceptron Model and its significance in the development of Neural Networks, Intelligent Virtual Assistants, and Deep Learning.

At its core, the Perceptron Model is a mathematical model that imitates the functioning of a biological neuron. This model is a fundamental building block for constructing more complex neural networks that can perform tasks ranging from image and speech recognition to natural language processing.

The Perceptron Model consists of inputs, weights, a bias term, and an activation function. The inputs represent the features or attributes of the data, while the weights determine the importance or relevance of each input. The bias term allows for fine-tuning of the model, enabling it to fit the data more accurately. The activation function introduces non-linearity and decides whether the neuron should fire or remain dormant based on the weighted sum of inputs and bias.

In the context of AI, the Perceptron Model plays a vital role in training neural networks. It uses a process called supervised learning, where the model is provided with labeled training data and adjusts its weights and biases iteratively to minimize the error between predicted and actual outputs. This process is known as gradient descent, and it enables the Perceptron Model to learn from examples and make accurate predictions on new, unseen data.

The Perceptron Model has found extensive applications in various AI domains. For instance, Intelligent Virtual Assistants, such as Siri and Alexa, utilize neural networks built on the Perceptron Model to understand and respond to human voice commands. Additionally, the advancements in Deep Learning owe their success to the Perceptron Model as it forms the foundation for training complex neural networks with multiple hidden layers.

Understanding the Perceptron Model is crucial for anyone interested in Artificial Intelligence, Machine Learning Algorithms, Neural Networks, Intelligent Virtual Assistants, or Deep Learning. It provides the necessary knowledge and tools to develop sophisticated AI systems capable of solving complex tasks and mimicking human-like intelligence.

In the subsequent chapters of this book, we will explore more advanced concepts and techniques that build upon the Perceptron Model, enabling you to further enhance your understanding and expertise in the field of AI.

Feedforward Neural Networks

In the rapidly evolving field of Artificial Intelligence (AI), one of the most significant breakthroughs has been the development of Feedforward Neural Networks. These networks, inspired by the human brain, have revolutionized the way machines learn and process information. In this subchapter, we will delve into the intricacies of Feedforward Neural Networks, their applications, and their impact on various domains.

At its core, a Feedforward Neural Network is a type of artificial neural network where information flows in a unidirectional manner, from the input layer to the output layer, without any feedback loops. This architecture allows the network to process complex data and make predictions or classifications based on learned patterns. Unlike traditional algorithms, which rely on explicit programming, Feedforward Neural Networks autonomously learn from data through a process called training.

The applications of Feedforward Neural Networks are vast and varied. In the realm of machine learning algorithms, they have been instrumental in solving problems such as image and speech recognition, natural language processing, and recommendation systems. These networks have also played a crucial role in the development of intelligent virtual assistants, enabling them to understand and respond to human language and commands with remarkable accuracy.

One of the key advantages of Feedforward Neural Networks is their ability to handle large-scale datasets and extract meaningful insights from them. This has made them indispensable in domains like healthcare, finance, and transportation, where large amounts of data are generated daily. By employing deep learning techniques, which involve multiple layers of interconnected neurons, these networks can uncover intricate patterns and relationships that might otherwise go unnoticed.

While the potential of Feedforward Neural Networks is immense, they come with their own set of challenges. Designing an optimal network architecture, selecting appropriate activation functions, and fine-tuning hyperparameters are some of the tasks that demand expertise and computational resources. Furthermore, the ethical implications of AI and its impact on privacy and job security need to be carefully considered and addressed.

In conclusion, Feedforward Neural Networks have emerged as a powerful tool in the field of AI, enabling machines to learn, adapt, and make intelligent decisions. Their impact can be witnessed in various domains, from intelligent virtual assistants to deep learning algorithms. As technology continues to advance, it is crucial for individuals over 30 to stay curious and keep abreast of these developments, ensuring that they can actively participate in the AI revolution and harness its potential for the betterment of society.

Convolutional Neural Networks

In the vast realm of Artificial Intelligence (AI) and Machine Learning (ML) algorithms, there exists a powerful and widely used technique known as Convolutional Neural Networks (CNNs). This subchapter aims to demystify the concept of CNNs and shed light on their significance in the field of AI and ML.

CNNs are a specific type of neural network architecture that have revolutionized various domains, including computer vision, image recognition, and natural language processing. They are designed to process data with a grid-like topology, such as images or time series data, by leveraging the power of deep learning.

One of the key advantages of CNNs is their ability to automatically learn and extract meaningful features from raw input data. This is achieved through the application of convolutional filters, which convolve across the input data, capturing spatial and temporal patterns. By stacking multiple convolutional layers, CNNs can progressively learn more complex and abstract representations of the input.

The application of CNNs in computer vision tasks has been particularly remarkable. From image classification and object detection to facial recognition and autonomous driving, CNNs have outperformed traditional approaches by a significant margin. Their ability to learn hierarchical features, combined with techniques such as pooling and dropout, has made CNNs highly adaptable to various real-world scenarios.

Furthermore, CNNs have paved the way for the development of intelligent virtual assistants, such as Siri, Alexa, and Google Assistant. By combining natural language processing and deep learning, these assistants can understand and respond to human queries with remarkable accuracy. CNNs play a crucial role in processing and extracting relevant information from the vast amount of textual and audio data they encounter.

As the field of AI continues to advance, CNNs remain at the forefront of research and development. With the advent of deep learning frameworks and powerful computing resources, training large-scale CNNs has become feasible, unlocking new possibilities in fields like healthcare, finance, and robotics.

In conclusion, Convolutional Neural Networks are a vital component of the AI and ML ecosystem. Their ability to automatically learn and extract meaningful features from grid-like data has transformed various domains. Whether it's image recognition, natural language processing, or building intelligent virtual assistants, CNNs have proven to be a game-changer. As the over 30's audience, understanding the fundamentals of CNNs is essential for staying informed about the latest advancements in AI and leveraging their potential in various industries.

Recurrent Neural Networks

In the world of Artificial Intelligence (AI), one of the most powerful tools at our disposal is the Recurrent Neural Network (RNN). This subchapter will delve into the intricacies of RNNs, explaining how they work and their applications in various fields such as machine learning algorithms, neural networks, intelligent virtual assistants, and deep learning.

RNNs are a type of artificial neural network that can process sequential data, making them particularly useful in tasks that involve predicting or generating sequences. Unlike traditional feedforward neural networks, which process one input at a time, RNNs have a hidden state that allows them to retain information from previous inputs. This characteristic enables RNNs to analyze and interpret data in a temporal context, making them ideal for tasks like speech recognition, natural language processing, and time series analysis.

One area where RNNs have shown remarkable success is in machine learning algorithms. By learning patterns and dependencies in sequential data, RNNs can make accurate predictions and generate meaningful outputs. For instance, in stock market predictions, RNNs can analyze historical price movements and provide insights into future trends. Similarly, in language modeling, RNNs can generate coherent and context-aware text by learning from large corpora of text data.

Furthermore, RNNs play a crucial role in the development of intelligent virtual assistants, such as Siri or Alexa. These assistants utilize RNN-based algorithms to understand and respond to user queries, making them more conversational and human-like in their interactions. RNNs enable virtual assistants to remember previous inputs and retain context, resulting in more accurate and personalized responses.

Deep learning, a subfield of AI that focuses on creating neural networks with multiple layers, heavily relies on RNNs. Deep RNN architectures, such as Long Short-Term Memory (LSTM) networks, have revolutionized fields like speech recognition and machine translation. LSTMs can effectively capture long-term dependencies in sequential data, addressing the vanishing gradient problem faced by traditional RNNs.

In conclusion, Recurrent Neural Networks are a powerful tool in the field of AI, with applications ranging from machine learning algorithms to intelligent virtual assistants, and deep learning. Their ability to process sequential data and retain information from previous inputs makes them indispensable in tasks that involve predicting or generating sequences. As the field of AI continues to advance, understanding and harnessing the power of RNNs will be crucial for anyone working in the niches of artificial intelligence, machine learning algorithms, neural networks, intelligent virtual assistants, and deep learning.

04

Chapter 4: Intelligent Virtual Assistants

What are Intelligent Virtual Assistants?

In today's era of technological advancements, intelligent virtual assistants have emerged as a groundbreaking application of artificial intelligence (AI) and machine learning algorithms. These sophisticated computer programs are designed to simulate human-like interactions and provide users with personalized assistance and support. Intelligent virtual assistants utilize neural networks and deep learning techniques to continuously learn and improve their performance, making them an indispensable tool for individuals of all ages, especially those over 30 who are curious to explore the world of AI.

Intelligent virtual assistants, commonly known as IVAs, are revolutionizing the way we interact with technology. Gone are the days when we had to navigate complex menus or rely on search engines to find information. IVAs offer a more natural and intuitive way of accessing information, performing tasks, and even engaging in casual conversations. Whether it's scheduling appointments, setting reminders, answering questions, or controlling smart home devices, these virtual assistants are always ready to assist.

The underlying technology behind IVAs is complex, relying heavily on machine learning algorithms and neural networks. Through continuous training and analysis of user data, these assistants become more intelligent and accurate in understanding and responding to human queries. Deep learning, a subset of machine learning, plays a crucial role in enabling IVAs to recognize patterns, understand context, and even predict user preferences.

One of the key advantages of IVAs is their ability to adapt to individual users. As they learn from user interactions, they can personalize their responses and recommendations, tailoring their assistance to meet the unique needs and preferences of each user. This level of personalization fosters a more engaging and efficient user experience, making IVAs an invaluable tool for busy professionals and individuals seeking convenience in their daily lives.

Intelligent virtual assistants are not limited to just personal use; they also have significant applications in business settings. From customer support to data analysis, IVAs can streamline processes, improve efficiency, and enhance overall productivity. By automating repetitive tasks and providing real-time insights, IVAs empower organizations to focus their resources on more complex and value-driven activities.

In conclusion, intelligent virtual assistants are an exciting manifestation of the immense potential of artificial intelligence and machine learning algorithms. With their ability to understand context, learn from data, and provide personalized assistance, IVAs are transforming the way we interact with technology. As the field of AI continues to evolve, these virtual assistants will undoubtedly become more sophisticated and indispensable, catering to the needs and interests of individuals over 30 and beyond.

How Intelligent Virtual Assistants Work

In today's fast-paced world, intelligent virtual assistants have become an integral part of our daily lives. These AI-powered assistants, such as Siri, Alexa, and Google Assistant, have revolutionized the way we interact with technology and have made our lives more convenient and efficient. In this subchapter, we will delve into the inner workings of these intelligent virtual assistants and explore how they operate.

At the heart of intelligent virtual assistants lies artificial intelligence (AI) and machine learning algorithms. These assistants are designed to mimic human-like interactions and understand natural language processing. By utilizing neural networks and deep learning, they can process vast amounts of data and learn from it to improve their performance over time.

The first step in the functioning of intelligent virtual assistants is speech recognition. They can listen to and understand spoken commands through the use of sophisticated algorithms. These algorithms convert the spoken words into text, which is then analyzed to identify the user's intent.

Next, the assistants employ natural language processing (NLP) techniques to decipher the meaning behind the user's command. NLP helps in understanding the context, intent, and sentiment of the user's query. This enables the assistants to provide accurate and relevant responses.

To generate the most appropriate response, intelligent virtual assistants utilize a combination of pre-programmed responses and machine learning. Initially, developers train the assistants with a vast amount of data to teach them how to respond to different types of queries. As the assistants interact with users, they continuously learn and adapt their responses based on user feedback and patterns in data.

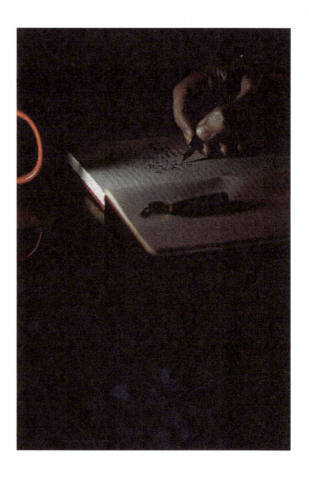

Deep learning plays a crucial role in enhancing the performance of intelligent virtual assistants. Through deep learning techniques, these assistants can analyze and understand complex patterns in data, enabling them to provide more accurate and personalized responses. This ability to learn and adapt allows the assistants to constantly improve their performance and provide better user experiences.

In addition to their ability to understand and respond to queries, intelligent virtual assistants can also interact with other devices and applications. Through integration with various APIs and platforms, they can perform tasks such as setting reminders, sending messages, playing music, and controlling smart home devices.

Intelligent virtual assistants have come a long way in a relatively short period. They have transformed the way we interact with technology and have become an indispensable tool in our daily lives. With ongoing advancements in AI and machine learning, these assistants will only continue to improve, providing us with even more personalized and efficient experiences.

Popular Intelligent Virtual Assistants in the Market

In today's digital age, intelligent virtual assistants have become a ubiquitous presence in our daily lives. These advanced AI-powered tools have revolutionized the way we interact with technology, providing us with personalized assistance and streamlined experiences. In this subchapter, we will explore some of the most popular intelligent virtual assistants available in the market today, catering to the curious minds of the over 30s.

1. Amazon Alexa: Developed by Amazon, Alexa has gained widespread popularity due to its integration with various smart devices. This intelligent virtual assistant can perform a multitude of tasks, such as answering questions, playing music, controlling home automation systems, and even ordering products online. With its constantly expanding skill set, Alexa continues to evolve and adapt to individual needs.

2. Google Assistant: Powered by Google's vast knowledge base and machine learning algorithms, Google Assistant is another prominent player in the virtual assistant market. It can perform a wide range of tasks, from setting reminders and sending messages to providing real-time weather updates and navigating through traffic. Its ability to understand context and deliver accurate information has made it a favorite among users.

3. Apple Siri: Siri, Apple's virtual assistant, has been a pioneer in the field since its introduction in 2011. Available on Apple devices, Siri can perform tasks, answer questions, and provide recommendations based on user preferences. With continuous improvements in natural language processing and deep learning, Siri has become increasingly efficient in understanding user commands and offering personalized responses.

4. Microsoft Cortana: Developed by Microsoft, Cortana is a virtual assistant integrated into the Windows operating system. It offers a range of features, including voice command recognition, schedule management, and third-party app integration. Cortana's integration with Microsoft's suite of products makes it a valuable tool for productivity and organization.

5. Samsung Bixby: Bixby is Samsung's intelligent virtual assistant, designed to enhance the user experience across its devices. Bixby's deep learning capabilities enable it to adapt to users' preferences and provide personalized recommendations. From controlling smart home devices to providing voice-guided assistance, Bixby aims to simplify and streamline daily tasks.

These are just a few examples of the popular intelligent virtual assistants available in the market. As AI, machine learning algorithms, neural networks, and deep learning continue to advance, we can expect further improvements in the capabilities of these virtual assistants. With their ability to understand human language, adapt to individual preferences, and perform a wide range of tasks, intelligent virtual assistants are transforming the way we interact with technology, making our lives more convenient and efficient.

Integration of Intelligent Virtual Assistants with AI Technologies

In today's rapidly evolving digital landscape, the integration of intelligent virtual assistants with AI technologies has revolutionized the way we interact with machines and access information. These advancements have significantly impacted various industries, from healthcare to finance, and have become an integral part of our daily lives. In this subchapter, we will explore the profound implications of this integration and its potential to shape the future of artificial intelligence, machine learning algorithms, neural networks, and deep learning.

Intelligent virtual assistants, such as Siri, Alexa, or Google Assistant, have become household names, offering convenience and efficiency through voice recognition and natural language processing. However, their capabilities go beyond answering simple queries or setting reminders. The integration with AI technologies has empowered these virtual assistants to learn and adapt, making them more intelligent and capable of complex tasks.

One of the key AI technologies driving this integration is machine learning algorithms. These algorithms enable virtual assistants to analyze vast amounts of data and identify patterns, allowing them to improve their understanding and responses over time. By continuously learning from user interactions and feedback, intelligent virtual assistants can provide personalized and contextually relevant information, enhancing their overall performance and user experience.

Neural networks, a subset of machine learning, play a vital role in the integration of intelligent virtual assistants with AI technologies. These networks mimic the human brain's structure and function, enabling virtual assistants to recognize and interpret speech, images, and even emotions. Through deep learning, neural networks can process and understand complex data, leading to more accurate and nuanced responses from virtual assistants.

The integration of intelligent virtual assistants with AI technologies also holds immense potential in transforming industries like healthcare. Virtual assistants can assist doctors by analyzing medical records, suggesting treatment plans, or even diagnosing diseases. Additionally, they can provide personalized health recommendations and reminders, empowering individuals to take control of their well-being.

As the field of AI progresses, the integration of intelligent virtual assistants with AI technologies is expected to further enhance their capabilities. From improved natural language processing to increased emotional intelligence, virtual assistants will become more human-like, enabling even more natural and seamless interactions.

In conclusion, the integration of intelligent virtual assistants with AI technologies has transformed the way we interact with machines and access information. With advancements in machine learning algorithms, neural networks, and deep learning, virtual assistants have become more intelligent, personalized, and capable of complex tasks. This integration has wide-ranging implications across various industries and holds the potential to shape the future of artificial intelligence. As individuals over 30, understanding and embracing these advancements will empower us to navigate the ever-changing digital landscape more effectively and take advantage of the numerous benefits offered by intelligent virtual assistants.

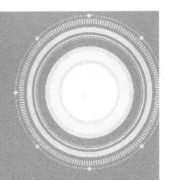

05

Chapter 5: Deep Learning and its Applications

Introduction to Deep Learning

In recent years, there has been a significant breakthrough in the field of Artificial Intelligence (AI) that has revolutionized the way machines learn and make decisions. This breakthrough is known as Deep Learning, and it has paved the way for incredible advancements in various domains, including machine learning algorithms, neural networks, and intelligent virtual assistants.

Deep Learning is a subset of machine learning that imitates the workings of the human brain in processing data and creating patterns for decision-making. It involves training artificial neural networks with vast amounts of labeled data, enabling them to recognize complex patterns and make accurate predictions or decisions.

This subchapter aims to introduce you to the fascinating world of Deep Learning and its applications. Whether you are new to the field or have some prior knowledge, this chapter will provide you with a comprehensive understanding of the fundamentals.

We will begin by exploring the basics of artificial neural networks, the building blocks of Deep Learning. You will learn about the different layers within a neural network and how they work together to process and analyze data. Understanding these layers is essential as they form the basis for more complex Deep Learning models.

Next, we will delve into the concept of machine learning algorithms and their relationship with Deep Learning. You will discover how Deep Learning algorithms differ from traditional machine learning algorithms and why they are particularly effective in handling unstructured data, such as images, text, and audio.

Furthermore, we will explore the practical applications of Deep Learning in various fields. From image and speech recognition to natural language processing and intelligent virtual assistants, you will see how Deep Learning has transformed these areas and paved the way for remarkable advancements.

Throughout this subchapter, we will also discuss the challenges and limitations of Deep Learning, as well as the ethical considerations surrounding its use. It is crucial to understand both the potential benefits and the responsible use of Deep Learning to ensure its positive impact on society.

By the end of this chapter, you will have a solid understanding of Deep Learning and its applications in the realm of Artificial Intelligence. Whether you are a professional seeking to expand your knowledge or simply a curious individual eager to explore the possibilities of AI, this subchapter will provide you with the necessary foundation to delve deeper into the world of Deep Learning.

Deep Learning Architectures

In the rapidly evolving field of Artificial Intelligence (AI), deep learning has emerged as a powerful approach to solving complex problems. This subchapter delves into the fascinating world of deep learning architectures, exploring the intricacies of neural networks and their applications in various domains.

Neural networks are at the heart of deep learning, mimicking the human brain's ability to process information and learn from it. These networks consist of interconnected layers of artificial neurons, each performing specific computations on input data. By training these networks on vast amounts of labeled data, they can extract patterns, make predictions, and perform tasks with remarkable accuracy.

One of the most widely used deep learning architectures is the Convolutional Neural Network (CNN), which has revolutionized computer vision. CNNs excel in image recognition, object detection, and even autonomous driving. They use convolutional layers to detect features in images and pooling layers to reduce the dimensions, enabling the network to learn hierarchical representations automatically.

Another notable architecture is the Recurrent Neural Network (RNN), which has proven effective in tasks involving sequential data, such as natural language processing and speech recognition. RNNs possess memory cells that allow them to remember and process information from previous steps, making them ideal for tasks requiring context and temporal dependencies.

As the demand for intelligent virtual assistants grows, deep learning architectures like the Long Short-Term Memory (LSTM) network have become essential. LSTMs are a variant of RNNs that excel in handling long-term dependencies and are widely used in speech recognition, language translation, and chatbots.

Advancements in deep learning have also led to the development of Generative Adversarial Networks (GANs). GANs consist of two neural networks: a generator and a discriminator. The generator creates synthetic data, while the discriminator tries to distinguish between real and fake data. This framework has found applications in image generation, video synthesis, and even creating realistic deepfake videos.

Understanding deep learning architectures is crucial for professionals in the AI and machine learning domains. By harnessing the power of neural networks, they can develop innovative solutions, automate complex tasks, and unlock the full potential of AI technology.

In conclusion, deep learning architectures, such as CNNs, RNNs, LSTMs, and GANs, have revolutionized the field of AI. They enable machines to learn from vast amounts of data, recognize patterns, and make accurate predictions. With applications ranging from computer vision to natural language processing, these architectures have become essential tools for researchers, engineers, and developers in the ever-expanding AI landscape. Embracing deep learning architectures empowers individuals to build intelligent systems and shape the future of technology.

Deep Learning for Image Recognition

In this subchapter, we will delve into the fascinating world of deep learning for image recognition. As the field of artificial intelligence continues to evolve, deep learning has emerged as a powerful tool for training machines to recognize and understand images, surpassing human-level performance in many cases. This technology has revolutionized various industries, from healthcare to autonomous vehicles, and understanding its fundamentals is crucial for anyone interested in the field of artificial intelligence.

Deep learning algorithms, inspired by the structure of the human brain's neural networks, have proven to be highly effective in image recognition tasks. These algorithms are designed to automatically learn and extract complex features from raw image data, enabling machines to understand and interpret visual information like never before. This has paved the way for advancements in areas such as object detection, facial recognition, and even medical imaging analysis.

Neural networks play a vital role in deep learning for image recognition. They consist of layers of interconnected nodes, or artificial neurons, that process and analyze image data at different levels of abstraction. By using large datasets, these networks can learn to recognize patterns and make accurate predictions based on the input images. Convolutional neural networks (CNNs), a specialized type of neural network, have been particularly successful in image recognition tasks and are widely used in various applications today.

One of the most exciting applications of deep learning for image recognition is the development of intelligent virtual assistants. These assistants, powered by advanced neural networks, can now accurately identify objects and understand natural language commands from users. This has opened up a world of possibilities for hands-free control of devices and personalized user experiences.

As an over 30's audience, it is essential to understand the potential impact of deep learning on various industries and our daily lives. From healthcare diagnostics to autonomous vehicles, the integration of deep learning algorithms in image recognition is transforming the way we interact with technology. By familiarizing ourselves with the concepts and techniques behind deep learning, we can better appreciate the capabilities and limitations of these powerful systems.

In the following sections of this subchapter, we will explore the underlying principles of deep learning for image recognition, including the architecture of neural networks, training methodologies, and the importance of large datasets. We will also discuss real-world applications, challenges, and ethical considerations associated with this rapidly advancing field.

Whether you are a curious individual seeking to understand the latest advancements in artificial intelligence or a professional looking to integrate image recognition into your work, this subchapter will provide invaluable insights into the world of deep learning for image recognition.

Deep Learning for Natural Language Processing

In recent years, the field of Artificial Intelligence (AI) has witnessed tremendous advancements, particularly in the realm of Natural Language Processing (NLP). This subchapter delves into the intersection of AI and NLP, with a focus on the groundbreaking technique of Deep Learning.

Deep Learning refers to a subset of machine learning algorithms that are inspired by the structure and function of the human brain's neural networks. These algorithms have revolutionized the way computers understand and process human language, enabling them to perform tasks such as language translation, sentiment analysis, speech recognition, and intelligent virtual assistants.

Natural Language Processing, on the other hand, involves the interaction between computers and human language. It encompasses a wide range of tasks, including text classification, information retrieval, and question-answering systems. Deep Learning algorithms have emerged as a powerful tool for tackling the complexities of NLP, surpassing traditional rule-based approaches.

One of the key advantages of Deep Learning for NLP is its ability to automatically learn features from raw data. This eliminates the need for manual feature engineering, where human experts painstakingly design and select relevant features. With Deep Learning, the algorithms can autonomously extract meaningful representations from large amounts of text data, leading to more accurate and robust models.

One notable application of Deep Learning in NLP is the development of intelligent virtual assistants like Siri, Alexa, and Google Assistant. These virtual assistants employ advanced Deep Learning models to understand spoken language, respond to queries, and perform tasks on behalf of the user. Through continuous learning and adaptation, these virtual assistants have become indispensable tools in our daily lives.

Moreover, Deep Learning has also revolutionized machine translation. Neural Machine Translation (NMT) models, based on Deep Learning, have outperformed traditional statistical approaches. These models can learn the semantic and syntactic relationships within languages, resulting in more accurate and fluent translations.

As an audience of over 30's, understanding the capabilities and implications of Deep Learning for NLP is crucial in today's AI-driven world. It opens up opportunities for career advancement, helps in better decision-making, and enables you to leverage cutting-edge technologies. Whether you are interested in building intelligent virtual assistants, improving language translation, or simply staying informed about the latest advancements in AI, exploring Deep Learning for NLP is an essential step towards AI mastery.

Deep Learning in Healthcare and Finance

Artificial Intelligence (AI) has revolutionized various industries, and two sectors that have greatly benefited from its advancements are healthcare and finance. Within these domains, deep learning has emerged as a powerful tool, enabling remarkable breakthroughs in diagnosis, treatment, risk assessment, fraud detection, and more. In this subchapter, we will explore the fascinating applications of deep learning in healthcare and finance, shedding light on its potential to transform these industries.

In healthcare, deep learning algorithms have demonstrated exceptional capabilities in medical imaging analysis, enabling more accurate and timely diagnoses. By training neural networks on vast amounts of medical imaging data, radiologists can now leverage intelligent systems to detect abnormalities, such as tumors, with higher precision. Deep learning also plays a crucial role in drug discovery and personalized medicine.

By analyzing large datasets, AI models can identify potential drug candidates and predict patient response to specific treatments, leading to more efficient and effective medical interventions.

Moving to the finance sector, deep learning algorithms are revolutionizing fraud detection and risk management. Financial institutions can employ these intelligent systems to analyze vast amounts of transactional data, identifying patterns indicative of fraudulent activities. This helps prevent monetary losses and safeguards customers' financial well-being. Additionally, deep learning algorithms can analyze market trends and predict stock prices, aiding investors in making informed decisions and mitigating potential risks.

Intelligent virtual assistants have also gained significant traction in both healthcare and finance. These virtual agents can provide personalized support to patients, offering real-time medical advice, monitoring vital signs, and reminding individuals to take medication. In finance, virtual assistants can assist customers in managing their finances, providing personalized recommendations, and answering queries related to investments, loans, and insurance.

While the potential of deep learning in healthcare and finance is immense, it is essential to address the associated ethical concerns. Privacy and security of sensitive health and financial data should be prioritized, ensuring that algorithms are transparent, fair, and accountable. Moreover, appropriate regulations and guidelines need to be established to govern the use of AI in these critical sectors, striking a balance between innovation and responsible deployment.

In conclusion, deep learning is revolutionizing healthcare and finance by empowering professionals with powerful AI tools. Its applications in medical imaging analysis, drug discovery, fraud detection, risk management, and virtual assistants are transforming these industries, enhancing accuracy, efficiency, and customer experience. However, ethical considerations and responsible implementation are crucial to ensure the integrity and privacy of sensitive data. As professionals in the AI, machine learning, neural networks, and deep learning niches, it is our responsibility to contribute to the ethical and sustainable advancement of these technologies, shaping a future where AI and humans work harmoniously to improve lives.

06

Chapter 6: Ethical Considerations in AI

Ethical Issues in Artificial Intelligence

Artificial Intelligence (AI) is rapidly transforming various aspects of our lives, including how we work, communicate, and make decisions. However, as AI continues to advance, it is essential to address the ethical concerns that arise in its development and deployment. This subchapter explores some of the key ethical issues in artificial intelligence and aims to provide insights for the curious minds of individuals aged 30 and above who are interested in the fields of AI, machine learning algorithms, neural networks, intelligent virtual assistants, and deep learning.

One of the critical ethical considerations in AI is the potential bias embedded in machine learning algorithms. AI systems are designed to learn from vast amounts of data, and if the training data is biased, the AI models may perpetuate and amplify existing societal biases. This can lead to discrimination in areas such as hiring, loan approvals, or criminal justice systems. It is crucial to ensure that AI models are trained on diverse and representative datasets to minimize such biases.

Another ethical concern is the impact of AI on employment. As AI technology advances, there is a legitimate fear that many jobs may become automated, leading to unemployment and economic inequality. The ethical challenge lies in finding ways to ensure a just transition for workers and to create new job opportunities that harness the unique skills and capabilities of humans.

Privacy is another significant concern in the era of AI. Intelligent virtual assistants, such as voice-activated devices, collect vast amounts of personal data to improve their functionality. However, this raises questions about consent, data storage, and potential misuse of personal information. Striking the right balance between AI's benefits and individual privacy rights is essential.

Moreover, the use of AI in autonomous vehicles raises ethical dilemmas. How should AI be programmed to make split-second decisions in life-threatening situations? Should it prioritize the safety of the vehicle's occupants or the pedestrians? These ethical considerations require careful thought and discussion to ensure that AI systems act in the best interest of society as a whole.

Lastly, transparency and accountability in AI decision-making are crucial. Deep learning models, which are highly complex and opaque, often make decisions that even their creators struggle to explain. This lack of transparency can lead to mistrust and hinder the adoption of AI systems. It is vital to develop tools and frameworks that enhance AI interpretability and accountability to address these concerns.

In conclusion, as AI continues to advance, it is essential to address the ethical issues that arise. By recognizing and discussing these concerns, individuals aged 30 and above with an interest in artificial intelligence, machine learning algorithms, neural networks, intelligent virtual assistants, and deep learning can actively contribute to shaping a responsible and beneficial future for AI.

Bias and Fairness in AI

As we delve into the fascinating world of artificial intelligence (AI) and its various applications, it becomes imperative to understand the potential biases that can emerge within these systems. AI algorithms, particularly those based on machine learning, neural networks, and deep learning, are designed to learn from vast amounts of data to make predictions and decisions. However, they are not immune to the biases that exist in our society.

Bias in AI can manifest in numerous ways, from subtle to overt, and can have significant consequences. It is crucial for individuals, especially those over 30 who are curious about AI, to be aware of these biases and strive for fairness in the development and deployment of AI systems.

One prominent form of bias in AI arises from biased data. Machine learning algorithms learn from historical data, and if the data is biased, the algorithm will reflect those biases in its predictions. For instance, if historical hiring data exhibits gender bias, an AI system trained on such data may unwittingly perpetuate the same bias when recommending candidates for a job. This can reinforce societal inequalities and limit opportunities for marginalized groups.

Moreover, biases can be introduced during the design and training phases of AI systems. The decisions made by engineers and data scientists, consciously or unconsciously, can influence the behavior and outcomes of AI algorithms. It is crucial for AI practitioners to be mindful of their own biases and actively work towards fairness and inclusivity.

Addressing bias in AI requires a multifaceted approach. Firstly, diverse and representative datasets should be used to train AI algorithms, ensuring that the data reflects the real-world population accurately. Additionally, regular audits and evaluations should be conducted to detect and mitigate any biases that may have crept into the system.

Furthermore, transparency and accountability are essential in the development and deployment of AI systems. Users should have access to information about how decisions are being made and be able to contest them if they suspect bias. Ethical guidelines and regulations can also play a significant role in promoting fairness in AI.

As the technology evolves, it is crucial for individuals over 30 with an interest in AI to stay informed about the latest advancements and be proactive in advocating for fairness and inclusivity. By recognizing and addressing biases in AI, we can ensure that these powerful technologies contribute positively to our society and do not inadvertently exacerbate existing inequalities.

In conclusion, bias and fairness in AI are critical topics that demand our attention. As we explore the realms of artificial intelligence, machine learning algorithms, neural networks, intelligent virtual assistants, and deep learning, it is essential to be aware of the biases that can permeate these systems. By striving for fairness, inclusivity, and transparency, we can harness the full potential of AI while minimizing the negative impacts of bias.

Privacy and Security Concerns

As artificial intelligence continues to advance and become an integral part of our lives, it is essential to address the privacy and security concerns associated with these technologies. While AI offers numerous benefits, it also raises valid questions about the potential risks and vulnerabilities that can arise.

One of the primary concerns surrounding AI is the collection and usage of personal data. Machine learning algorithms rely heavily on data, and to provide accurate and personalized experiences, they require access to vast amounts of information. This raises concerns about the privacy of individuals, as their personal data may be stored, analyzed, and potentially shared without their explicit consent.

It is crucial for users to understand how their data is being used and have control over its usage.

Neural networks, the backbone of many AI systems, are complex and opaque in nature. They make decisions based on patterns and correlations within the data, making it difficult to understand how they arrive at their conclusions. This lack of transparency raises concerns about accountability and bias. If the underlying data used to train these networks is flawed or biased, it can lead to discriminatory outcomes. It is essential to ensure that AI systems are fair, transparent, and accountable to prevent any unintended consequences.

Intelligent virtual assistants, such as Siri or Alexa, have become prevalent in households worldwide. While they offer convenience and assist in various tasks, they also pose potential risks to our privacy. These assistants constantly listen for activation keywords, which means they are constantly recording and analyzing conversations in our homes. This raises concerns about the security of personal conversations and the potential for unauthorized access or misuse of this data.

Deep learning, a subset of AI, relies on vast amounts of data and computing power. This creates a significant demand for storage and processing capabilities, which can result in security vulnerabilities. Hackers may exploit these vulnerabilities to gain access to sensitive data or manipulate AI systems for malicious purposes. It is crucial to implement robust security measures to protect AI infrastructure and data from potential threats.

To address these concerns, policymakers, researchers, and businesses need to work together to establish clear regulations and ethical guidelines for the development and deployment of AI technologies. Transparency must be prioritized to ensure that individuals have a clear understanding of how their data is being used. Additionally, AI systems should be regularly audited to identify and mitigate any biases or discriminatory outcomes.

In conclusion, as AI continues to evolve and integrate into our lives, it is essential to be aware of the privacy and security concerns associated with these technologies. By addressing these concerns proactively and implementing appropriate safeguards, we can harness the power of AI while protecting the rights and security of individuals in this digital age.

Transparency and Accountability in AI Systems

In the rapidly advancing world of Artificial Intelligence (AI), the need for transparency and accountability in AI systems has become paramount. As AI technologies such as machine learning algorithms, neural networks, intelligent virtual assistants, and deep learning continue to permeate various aspects of our lives, it is crucial for individuals, organizations, and society as a whole to understand and address the ethical implications surrounding these technologies.

Transparency in AI systems refers to the ability to understand how these systems make decisions and predictions. It is essential for users to have access to information about the underlying data, algorithms, and models used in AI systems. Without transparency, AI systems can become black boxes, making it difficult to trust their outputs or identify potential biases and errors. As the audience of "AI Mastery: A Guide for the Curious 30+ Mind," it is important for you to be aware of the importance of demanding transparency from AI developers and policymakers.

Accountability, on the other hand, refers to the responsibility and liability for the actions and decisions made by AI systems. As AI systems become increasingly autonomous, it becomes crucial to establish mechanisms for holding them accountable for their actions. In cases where AI systems are involved in critical decision-making processes, such as healthcare or criminal justice, the consequences of errors or bias could be severe. Therefore, implementing accountability measures, such as regulatory frameworks and auditing processes, becomes essential.

To ensure transparency and accountability in AI systems, various strategies can be adopted. Firstly, developers should prioritize explainable AI, which allows users to understand how the system arrived at its conclusions. This involves using interpretable machine learning algorithms and designing AI systems that provide explanations for their decisions.

Secondly, efforts should be made to address biases in AI systems. Machine learning algorithms are trained on historical data, which can inadvertently embed bias. It is crucial to critically analyze the training data and mitigate any discriminatory outcomes.

Lastly, policymakers and regulatory bodies should work hand in hand with AI developers to establish guidelines and standards for transparency and accountability. This includes mandating the disclosure of important information about the AI system, setting up mechanisms for auditing and monitoring AI systems, and creating avenues for redress in the event of harm caused by AI systems.

By fostering transparency and accountability in AI systems, we can ensure that these technologies are developed and deployed in a manner that benefits society as a whole. As an audience interested in artificial intelligence, machine learning algorithms, neural networks, intelligent virtual assistants, and deep learning, it is crucial to stay informed and advocate for responsible AI practices. Together, we can shape a future where AI systems are transparent, accountable, and aligned with our values and ethical standards.

Chapter 7: Implementing AI Solutions

Planning an AI Project

When embarking on an AI project, it is crucial to have a well-thought-out plan in place. This subchapter will guide you through the key steps involved in planning an AI project, ensuring that you set yourself up for success.

The first step is to clearly define your project goals. What problem are you trying to solve? How can artificial intelligence help you achieve those goals? By having a clear understanding of your objectives, you can better align your project with the desired outcomes.

Next, you need to identify the specific AI techniques that are most relevant to your project. Artificial intelligence encompasses a wide range of technologies, including machine learning algorithms, neural networks, intelligent virtual assistants, and deep learning. Understanding the strengths and limitations of each technique will help you determine which ones are most suitable for your project.

Once you have identified the appropriate AI techniques, it is essential to gather the necessary data. Data is the fuel that powers AI algorithms, and having high-quality, relevant data is crucial for accurate and reliable results. Consider what data you need and how you can acquire it. You may need to collect new data, clean existing data, or collaborate with other organizations to gain access to the required data.

With your goals defined and data gathered, the next step is to design and develop your AI model. This involves selecting the right algorithms, configuring the neural network architecture, and training the model on your data. It is important to allocate sufficient time and resources for this step, as it lays the foundation for your AI project's success.

Once your model is developed, you need to evaluate its performance. This involves testing the model on unseen data and measuring its accuracy and efficiency. It is crucial to conduct rigorous testing to ensure that your model performs well in real-world scenarios.

Finally, you need to plan for the deployment and maintenance of your AI project. Consider how the model will be integrated into your existing systems and how it will be updated and maintained over time. Additionally, think about the potential ethical and legal implications of your AI project and ensure compliance with relevant regulations.

By following these steps and planning your AI project meticulously, you increase the likelihood of achieving your desired outcomes. Remember, successful AI projects require careful planning, continuous learning, and adaptability to the ever-evolving field of artificial intelligence.

Data Collection and Preparation

In the world of Artificial Intelligence (AI) and its related fields such as Machine Learning Algorithms, Neural Networks, Intelligent Virtual Assistants, and Deep Learning, data collection and preparation are fundamental steps that cannot be overlooked. Whether you are a curious over 30-year-old looking to delve into these exciting technologies or a seasoned professional in the field, understanding the importance of data collection and preparation is crucial for success.

Data collection forms the backbone of any AI project. It involves gathering relevant and reliable data from various sources, such as databases, websites, sensors, or even social media platforms. The quality, quantity, and diversity of the data collected play a vital role in the performance and accuracy of AI systems. Therefore, it is essential to ensure that the collected data is representative of the problem domain and covers a wide range of scenarios.

However, data collection alone is not sufficient. Proper data preparation is equally critical to ensure that the collected data is clean, organized, and ready for analysis. This involves several steps, including data cleaning, feature selection, and data normalization. Data cleaning removes any inconsistencies, errors, or outliers that may affect the performance of AI algorithms.

Feature selection involves identifying the most relevant attributes or variables that contribute to the problem at hand, while data normalization ensures that all data is on a consistent scale.

To simplify the data collection and preparation process, various tools and techniques are available. These include web scraping tools, data extraction algorithms, and data preprocessing libraries. Leveraging these resources can help automate and streamline the data collection and preparation tasks, saving time and effort.

Furthermore, it is important to consider ethical considerations when collecting and preparing data. Privacy and security issues must be carefully addressed to ensure the protection of individuals' rights and sensitive information.

In summary, data collection and preparation are vital steps in the world of AI. They lay the foundation for developing accurate and reliable AI models and systems. By understanding the importance of proper data collection and preparation, curious over 30-year-olds and professionals alike can embark on their AI journey with confidence, knowing that they have a solid starting point for their projects.

Model Development and Training

In the ever-evolving landscape of technology, one field that has gained significant traction is Artificial Intelligence (AI). With its potential to revolutionize various industries, AI has become a topic of great interest for individuals over the age of 30. This subchapter, titled "Model Development and Training," delves into the intricate world of AI and provides insights into the key components of AI development, specifically focusing on machine learning algorithms, neural networks, intelligent virtual assistants, and deep learning.

Machine learning algorithms serve as the foundation of AI systems, enabling them to learn from data and make informed decisions. This subchapter explores the different types of machine learning algorithms, including supervised, unsupervised, and reinforcement learning, and the role they play in developing intelligent AI models. By understanding these algorithms, individuals over 30 can gain a deeper appreciation for the inner workings of AI and its potential applications in their respective fields.

Neural networks, inspired by the human brain, are another essential aspect of AI. This subchapter explains the structure and functionality of neural networks, highlighting their ability to process complex patterns and make accurate predictions. By grasping the concepts behind neural networks, readers can comprehend how AI systems can recognize images, understand natural language, and even generate creative content.

Intelligent virtual assistants, such as Siri and Alexa, have become an integral part of our daily lives. This subchapter explores the development of these virtual assistants, shedding light on the underlying AI technologies that enable them to understand and respond to human commands. By gaining insights into the architecture and training processes of these virtual assistants, readers can appreciate the advancements in natural language processing and its potential impact on various industries.

Lastly, deep learning, a subfield of machine learning, has garnered considerable attention for its ability to process vast amounts of data and extract meaningful insights. This subchapter delves into the principles of deep learning, discussing neural networks with multiple hidden layers and their ability to handle complex tasks like image recognition and language translation. By understanding the power of deep learning, individuals over 30 can envision the future of AI and its potential to transform industries such as healthcare, finance, and transportation.

In summary, this subchapter provides a comprehensive overview of model development and training in the field of AI. By exploring machine learning algorithms, neural networks, intelligent virtual assistants, and deep learning, individuals over 30 can gain a deeper understanding of AI's capabilities and its potential impact on society. Whether you are a curious mind or a seasoned professional, this subchapter will broaden your knowledge of AI and inspire you to embrace the possibilities of this transformative technology.

Testing and Evaluation

In the rapidly evolving field of Artificial Intelligence (AI), testing and evaluation play a crucial role in ensuring the reliability and effectiveness of various AI technologies such as machine learning algorithms, neural networks, intelligent virtual assistants, and deep learning models. This subchapter explores the significance of testing and evaluation in AI and provides insights into best practices for achieving optimal results.

Testing AI systems is essential to identify and rectify any flaws or shortcomings before they are deployed in real-world scenarios. It involves assessing the performance, accuracy, and robustness of AI algorithms and models. By subjecting AI systems to rigorous testing, developers can uncover potential biases, vulnerabilities, and limitations, ensuring that the technology is fair, unbiased, and reliable.

One of the primary testing methods employed in AI is using large datasets to train and validate machine learning algorithms and neural networks. These datasets consist of labeled examples that enable the algorithms to learn and make accurate predictions or classifications. Testing the trained models on separate datasets helps evaluate their generalization capabilities and measure their accuracy and performance.

However, testing AI systems goes beyond mere accuracy. It also involves evaluating their behavior in real-world scenarios and assessing their ethical implications. AI technologies, such as intelligent virtual assistants, must be tested to ensure they respect user privacy and maintain confidentiality. Additionally, developers must evaluate the potential risks associated with AI algorithms, such as unintended consequences or malicious exploitation.

To ensure effective testing and evaluation, it is crucial to establish comprehensive evaluation metrics that align with the specific AI technology being developed. For instance, in natural language processing tasks, metrics like precision, recall, and F1 score are commonly used to evaluate the performance of intelligent virtual assistants. Similarly, for image recognition tasks, metrics like accuracy and mean average precision are employed.

Furthermore, continuous monitoring and evaluation of AI systems post-deployment are vital to identify any performance degradation or changes in user behavior. This enables developers to adapt and improve the AI technology over time, ensuring its continued effectiveness and relevance.

In conclusion, testing and evaluation are integral components of the AI development lifecycle. Thorough testing ensures the accuracy, reliability, and ethical considerations of AI systems, while evaluation metrics help measure their performance and align them with their intended objectives. By embracing best practices in testing and evaluation, developers can harness the full potential of AI technologies, empowering them to create innovative solutions that benefit society as a whole.

Deployment and Maintenance of AI Solutions

As the field of Artificial Intelligence (AI) continues to evolve and revolutionize various industries, understanding the deployment and maintenance of AI solutions has become crucial for professionals in the 30+ age group. In this subchapter, we will explore key concepts related to deploying and maintaining AI solutions, providing valuable insights for those interested in Artificial Intelligence, machine learning algorithms, neural networks, intelligent virtual assistants, and deep learning.

When it comes to deploying AI solutions, it is essential to have a clear understanding of the organization's goals and objectives. This involves identifying problem areas that can benefit from AI, such as optimizing processes, improving customer experiences, or enhancing decision-making capabilities. Understanding these goals will help in selecting the right AI technologies and algorithms for the deployment process.

Machine learning algorithms play a vital role in AI solutions. These algorithms enable machines to learn from data and make accurate predictions or decisions. Understanding the different types of algorithms, such as supervised learning, unsupervised learning, and reinforcement learning, is crucial in choosing the most appropriate one for specific tasks. Additionally, knowledge of neural networks, which mimic the human brain, is essential for building and training advanced AI models.

Intelligent virtual assistants have gained significant popularity in recent years, making them a key area of focus for professionals. These virtual assistants, such as Siri or Alexa, use natural language processing and machine learning algorithms to understand and respond to user queries. Understanding the deployment and maintenance of intelligent virtual assistants is crucial for professionals looking to leverage this technology in their organizations.

Deep learning, a subset of machine learning, has emerged as a powerful technique for solving complex problems. It involves training neural networks with multiple layers to process vast amounts of data and make accurate predictions. Understanding the nuances of deep learning, including the architecture of deep neural networks and optimization techniques, is crucial for successfully deploying and maintaining AI solutions.

In addition to deployment, maintaining AI solutions is essential for continued success. This involves monitoring the performance of AI models, updating them with new data, and retraining them to ensure accuracy and relevancy. Moreover, ensuring the ethical use and unbiased nature of AI solutions is crucial to avoid potential risks and biases.

In conclusion, this subchapter has provided valuable insights into the deployment and maintenance of AI solutions. Professionals in the 30+ age group interested in Artificial Intelligence, machine learning algorithms, neural networks, intelligent virtual assistants, and deep learning can now leverage this knowledge to effectively implement and manage AI solutions in their respective industries. By understanding the goals, algorithms, virtual assistants, and deep learning techniques, professionals can stay ahead in this rapidly evolving field.

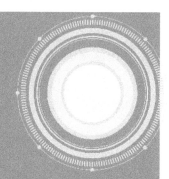

08

Chapter 8: Future Trends in AI

Advancements in Artificial Intelligence

In recent years, the world has witnessed an unprecedented surge in advancements in the field of Artificial Intelligence (AI). This subchapter explores the remarkable progress made in various areas, such as machine learning algorithms, neural networks, intelligent virtual assistants, and deep learning. As we delve into these topics, we aim to provide a comprehensive understanding of the cutting-edge developments that have taken place in the AI landscape.

Machine learning algorithms lie at the heart of AI, enabling computers to learn and make predictions without being explicitly programmed. Over the past decade, significant breakthroughs have been achieved in this domain, allowing machines to process vast amounts of data and derive meaningful insights. These algorithms have revolutionized various industries, including healthcare, finance, and transportation, by enhancing decision-making processes and enabling the automation of complex tasks.

Neural networks, inspired by the human brain's structure and functioning, have also undergone remarkable advancements. These complex networks of interconnected nodes, or artificial neurons, have been instrumental in solving problems that were previously considered unsolvable. Neural networks have demonstrated unparalleled capabilities in image recognition, natural language processing, and even autonomous driving, revolutionizing industries such as healthcare, retail, and manufacturing.

Intelligent virtual assistants, powered by AI, have become an integral part of our daily lives. From Siri to Google Assistant and Amazon's Alexa, these voice-activated assistants have become increasingly sophisticated, understanding and responding to human queries in a more natural and intuitive manner. These virtual assistants assist us in managing our schedules, providing recommendations, and even controlling smart devices in our homes.

Deep learning, a subset of machine learning, has gained immense popularity due to its ability to process and analyze vast amounts of unstructured data, such as images, videos, and text. This technology has had a significant impact on fields like computer vision, natural language processing, and robotics. Deep learning algorithms have enabled machines to recognize objects, understand human speech, and even mimic human-like behaviors.

As AI continues to evolve rapidly, it holds tremendous potential to transform various industries and improve our daily lives. However, it is crucial to acknowledge the ethical considerations associated with these advancements, such as privacy concerns and potential job displacement. In this subchapter, we aim to shed light on these issues and encourage a thoughtful and responsible approach to the adoption of AI technologies.

In conclusion, the advancements in artificial intelligence have opened up new frontiers of possibilities. From machine learning algorithms and neural networks to intelligent virtual assistants and deep learning, these technologies have the potential to reshape industries and redefine how we interact with technology. By staying informed about these advancements, the curious 30+ mind can actively participate in the AI revolution, ensuring that its potential benefits are harnessed while addressing the challenges it presents.

Impact of AI on Different Industries

In recent years, the rapid advancement of Artificial Intelligence (AI) has had a profound impact on various industries, revolutionizing the way businesses operate and transforming the world as we know it. From healthcare to finance, transportation to manufacturing, AI is reshaping every aspect of our lives. This subchapter explores the far-reaching implications of AI on different industries and highlights the potential benefits and challenges associated with its implementation.

One industry that has witnessed significant transformation due to AI is healthcare. Intelligent virtual assistants powered by machine learning algorithms and neural networks have revolutionized patient care, enabling more accurate diagnoses and personalized treatment plans. AI algorithms can analyze vast amounts of medical data to detect patterns and predict diseases, leading to early intervention and improved patient outcomes. Furthermore, AI-powered robots can assist in surgeries, enhancing precision and reducing human error.

The finance industry has also embraced AI to enhance efficiency and improve decision-making. Machine learning algorithms are employed to analyze market trends and predict stock prices, enabling traders to make informed investment choices. AI-powered chatbots provide personalized customer service, answering queries and resolving issues promptly. Additionally, AI algorithms can detect fraudulent activities in real-time, minimizing financial fraud and ensuring the security of transactions.

Transportation is another sector experiencing significant disruption through AI. Autonomous vehicles, enabled by deep learning and neural networks, are poised to revolutionize the way we travel. These vehicles can navigate through complex traffic situations, reducing accidents and improving road safety. AI algorithms can optimize traffic flow, minimizing congestion and promoting efficient transportation systems.

The manufacturing industry has also embraced AI to optimize production processes. AI-powered robots and machines can automate repetitive and labor-intensive tasks, leading to increased productivity and reduced costs. Machine learning algorithms can analyze sensor data to predict equipment failures, enabling proactive maintenance and minimizing downtime. Furthermore, AI algorithms can optimize supply chain management, ensuring timely delivery of goods and reducing inventory costs.

While the impact of AI on different industries is undoubtedly transformative, it also presents challenges. Ethical considerations, such as data privacy and algorithmic bias, need to be addressed to ensure AI benefits all segments of society. Additionally, the potential displacement of jobs due to automation requires careful planning and retraining of the workforce.

In conclusion, AI has the potential to revolutionize various industries, transforming the way we live and work. From healthcare to finance, transportation to manufacturing, the applications of AI are limitless. However, it is crucial to navigate the ethical implications and address potential challenges to ensure AI is harnessed for the benefit of all.

Challenges and Opportunities in AI

Artificial Intelligence (AI) has captivated the interest of people across various industries, and for good reason. This subchapter delves into the challenges and opportunities that AI presents, specifically targeting the over 30's audience interested in Artificial Intelligence, Machine Learning Algorithms, Neural Networks, Intelligent Virtual Assistants, and Deep Learning.

One of the primary challenges in AI is the ethical dilemma it poses. As AI becomes more sophisticated, questions arise about its impact on employment. Will AI replace human jobs? How do we ensure that AI is used ethically and responsively? These are crucial concerns that require careful consideration and proactive measures.

Another challenge is the bias in AI algorithms. AI systems learn from the data they are fed, which can lead to biased decision-making. This bias can be harmful and discriminatory, affecting various aspects of our lives, including hiring practices, healthcare, and criminal justice. The over 30's audience is well-aware of the importance of fairness, equality, and diversity and will find this topic particularly engaging.

Despite these challenges, AI offers numerous opportunities for innovation and advancement. Machine Learning Algorithms allow AI systems to learn and improve from data, enabling them to make accurate predictions and assist in decision-making processes. Neural Networks mimic the human brain and have the potential to revolutionize various fields, such as healthcare, finance, and transportation.

Intelligent Virtual Assistants like Siri, Alexa, and Google Assistant have become an integral part of our daily lives, simplifying tasks and providing personalized recommendations. The over 30's audience, with their busy lifestyles, will appreciate the convenience and efficiency that intelligent virtual assistants bring.

Deep Learning, a subset of Machine Learning, focuses on training AI systems to analyze and interpret complex patterns. This technology has the potential to revolutionize industries such as healthcare, finance, and cybersecurity, providing more accurate diagnoses, predicting market trends, and enhancing data security.

In conclusion, AI presents both challenges and opportunities that demand our attention. Ethical considerations, bias in algorithms, and potential job displacement are some of the challenges to overcome. However, the opportunities for innovation, improved decision-making, and personalized assistance are vast. The over 30's audience, with their wealth of experience and curiosity, will find this subchapter enlightening and thought-provoking as they navigate the evolving world of AI.

Predictions for the Future of AI

A little space to be creative

As we enter the age of artificial intelligence (AI), it is essential for the curious minds of the over 30s to understand the potential and implications of this revolutionary technology. AI Mastery: A Guide for the Curious 30+ Mind explores the future of AI, providing insights into various aspects such as machine learning algorithms, neural networks, intelligent virtual assistants, and deep learning. In this subchapter, we delve into the predictions for the future of AI, giving you a glimpse of what lies ahead.

The first prediction is the continued advancement of machine learning algorithms. As AI systems gather more data and learn from user interactions, they will become more accurate and efficient. This will lead to increased automation in various industries, improving productivity and streamlining processes. Machine learning algorithms will enable businesses to make data-driven decisions, enhancing their competitiveness and driving innovation.

Neural networks, the backbone of AI, will also undergo significant developments. The future will witness the creation of more complex and sophisticated neural networks, capable of solving complex problems and mimicking human cognitive abilities. This will lead to breakthroughs in areas such as image recognition, natural language processing, and autonomous vehicles, transforming industries such as healthcare, transportation, and finance.

Intelligent virtual assistants, such as Siri and Alexa, will become even more intelligent and integrated into our daily lives. These assistants will evolve to understand context and emotions, offering personalized recommendations and anticipating our needs. Voice interfaces will become the primary mode of interaction, replacing traditional graphical interfaces, making technology more accessible and intuitive for everyone.

Deep learning, a subset of machine learning, will continue to push the boundaries of AI. Deep neural networks will enable machines to learn from unstructured data, unlocking new possibilities in areas like healthcare diagnosis, drug discovery, and personalized medicine. With deep learning, machines will be capable of analyzing vast amounts of data, spotting patterns, and making predictions with unparalleled accuracy.

However, along with these advancements, it is crucial to address the ethical considerations and potential risks associated with AI. As AI becomes more integrated into our lives, issues such as privacy, bias, and job displacement must be carefully managed to ensure a fair and inclusive future.

In conclusion, the future of AI holds immense promise and potential. Machine learning algorithms, neural networks, intelligent virtual assistants, and deep learning will continue to evolve, revolutionizing industries and transforming how we live and work. AI Mastery: A Guide for the Curious 30+ Mind equips you with the knowledge to navigate this exciting future, empowering you to embrace and benefit from the wonders of AI while addressing the challenges it presents. Stay curious, stay informed, and prepare yourself for the AI-driven world of tomorrow.

09

Chapter 9:
Conclusion

Recap of Key Concepts

In this subchapter, we will summarize the key concepts covered throughout the book "AI Mastery: A Guide for the Curious 30+ Mind." As an audience of over 30s who are interested in topics like Artificial Intelligence, Machine Learning Algorithms, Neural Networks, Intelligent Virtual Assistants, and Deep Learning, it is essential to have a clear understanding of these fundamental concepts.

Artificial Intelligence, commonly known as AI, refers to the development of computer systems that can perform tasks that typically require human intelligence. These tasks include speech recognition, decision-making, problem-solving, and language translation. AI has significantly impacted various industries, including healthcare, finance, and transportation.

Machine Learning Algorithms are the driving force behind AI systems. They are designed to enable computers to learn from and analyze large datasets without being explicitly programmed. Machine learning algorithms can identify patterns, make predictions, and discover insights from data, leading to faster and more accurate decision-making processes.

Neural Networks are a key component of machine learning algorithms. They are inspired by the human brain and consist of interconnected nodes called neurons. These networks are capable of learning and adapting by adjusting the strength of connections between neurons. Neural networks have revolutionized various fields, including image recognition, natural language processing, and autonomous vehicles.

Intelligent Virtual Assistants, such as Siri, Alexa, and Google Assistant, have become ubiquitous in our daily lives. These assistants use AI technologies to understand and respond to human voice commands and perform tasks like setting reminders, answering questions, and controlling smart home devices. The advancements in natural language processing and machine learning have made these virtual assistants more conversational and personalized.

Deep Learning is a subset of machine learning that focuses on training artificial neural networks with multiple layers. These deep neural networks can process and analyze complex data structures, such as images, audio, and text, achieving remarkable accuracy in tasks like image recognition, speech synthesis, and language translation.

Understanding these key concepts is crucial for harnessing the power of AI and staying relevant in today's technology-driven world. Whether you are a business professional, a researcher, or simply curious about the potential of AI, this book has provided you with a solid foundation to explore and embrace the advancements in Artificial Intelligence, Machine Learning Algorithms, Neural Networks, Intelligent Virtual Assistants, and Deep Learning. Keep learning, experimenting, and embracing the opportunities that AI offers, and you will undoubtedly be well-equipped for the future.

Final Thoughts and Recommendations for Further Learning

As we conclude this journey into the intricate world of AI, it is crucial for us, the curious 30+ minds, to reflect upon the knowledge we have gained and chart a path for further exploration. Artificial Intelligence, machine learning algorithms, neural networks, intelligent virtual assistants, and deep learning are areas that hold immense potential for our generation. Here are some final thoughts and recommendations to guide you on your continued quest for AI mastery.

Firstly, embrace the concept of lifelong learning. The field of AI is continuously evolving, and staying up-to-date with the latest advancements is essential. Make learning a habit by dedicating a set amount of time each week to explore new research papers, attend webinars, or enroll in online courses. This commitment to continual education will ensure you remain at the forefront of AI developments.

Next, consider specializing in one or more niches within AI. The vastness of AI can be overwhelming, so focusing on specific areas will allow you to deepen your understanding and expertise. Whether it's machine learning algorithms, neural networks, intelligent virtual assistants, or deep learning, choose a niche that aligns with your interests and invest time in mastering its intricacies.

Building practical skills is equally crucial. Theory alone will not suffice in the field of AI. Take advantage of open-source tools and platforms to gain hands-on experience. Experiment with coding machine learning models, develop your own neural networks, or create intelligent virtual assistants. The more you practice, the more confident you will become in implementing AI solutions.

Additionally, seek opportunities to collaborate and network with like-minded individuals. Join AI communities, attend conferences, and engage in discussions with experts in the field. Collaborative projects and sharing ideas will not only enrich your knowledge but also provide a platform for mutual growth and innovation.

Lastly, do not overlook the ethical considerations surrounding AI. As the technology becomes more powerful, it is our responsibility to ensure its ethical use. Stay informed about the ethical implications of AI and actively contribute to discussions on privacy, bias, and fairness. By promoting responsible AI practices, we can build a future where AI benefits humanity as a whole.

In conclusion, AI mastery is a continuous journey that requires dedication, specialization, practical skills, collaboration, and ethical awareness. Embrace the concept of lifelong learning, choose your niche, develop practical skills, collaborate with others, and prioritize ethical considerations. By following these recommendations, you will be well-equipped to navigate the ever-evolving landscape of AI and contribute meaningfully to its advancements. Remember, AI is not just a technology, but a force that has the potential to shape the future of humanity.

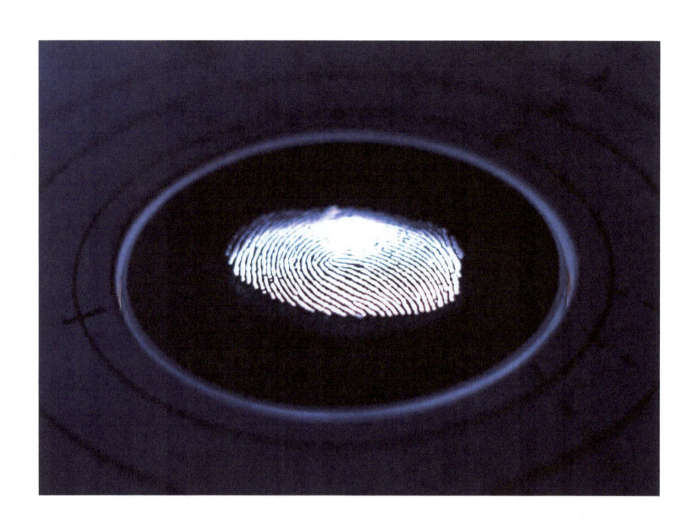